TINA'S TRADITIONAL BOOK OF SCONES

Tina shares her Traditional family recipes
from four generations of home bakers

TINA JESSON

Copyright © 2020 Tina Jesson. All rights reserved.

Edited by: Jillian Hinds-Williams

The right of Tina Jesson to be identified as the author of this work has been asserted by her in accordance with the Copyright, Designs and Patents Act 1988.

Visit: TinasTraditional.com

All rights reserved. The use of any part of this publication, reproduction, transmission in any form or by any means, electronic, mechanical, photocopying, recording or otherwise, or storage in a retrieval system, without the prior consent of the publisher is an infringement of the copyright law and is forbidden.

First edition publishing in 2014

This Special Edition hardback published worldwide in 2020

ISBN: 978-1-910853-24-5

Published by:

Lioness Publishing

LionessPublishing.com

facebook.com/LionessPublishing

instagram.com/LionessPublishing

twitter.com/lionesspublish

DEDICATION

This book is dedicated to the three ladies in my life who helped raise me, taught me how to become independent, how to have an insanely strong work ethic and who taught me how to cook, bake and make amazing preserves.

Little did I appreciate what they were teaching me when I was a child.

To my Mum, Vera Gerrard (nee Wren) and who I miss every day. Mum was a great pastry maker. Her cold hands made the greatest short crust, a technique I now teach to my team and to home bakers in bake classes.

Mum was born and raised in the village of Bradley Near Ashbourne, Derbyshire, England which is about 100 miles north of London, right in the center of the country. In fact my family owned the same property there for over 5 generations

To my Grandmother Wilhelmina (Jenny) Wren (nee Wooley) who was a great jam and preserves maker and whose Green Tomato Chutney recipe I sought out for the tearoom and a recipe we still use today.

My Great Grandmother, Gladys Wooley, who was born in 1899 and was a scullery maid at Bradley Hall at the time of Downton Abbey. She told me stories from the sinking of the titanic, through the time of the Great War and how she sheltered evacuee children in the second World War. These are the stories I now share in the Legacy Experiences I create with people from around the world.

The memories of their struggles and their humble lives keep me grounded every day and I was lucky enough to be raised by all 3 of them and am so proud of them and my British heritage.

ACKNOWLEDGMENTS

Dave, my husband of over 30 years. Don't know how he's put up with me for so long. For his faith in me, my cooking and my tearoom business and for being chief taster for all my recipes.

My kids, Daniel and Emma for getting roped in at every moment and listening to my ramblings, thanks for your support – even though I know your eyes have rolled from time to time.

The warm and wonderful people of Indiana for welcoming me, as I made my home far from my native England and for not only trying out my food, but for encouraging me to continue baking for them, and for clearing their plates every time.

My business coach Janie Sterling, for showing me I have what it takes, even when I have a wobble and lose confidence in myself.

My editor and good friend Jillian Hinds-Williams, for having patience with me and my poor spelling over the years and for understanding that I can cook much better than I can write. For having the faith in me to keep working on projects with me after over 30 years and helping me edit and publish this book. Thank you!

Image Credits:

All Photographs by Tina Jesson

In addition:

Herby Scones - Annie Mole - https://www.flickr.com/photos/anniemole/

Blueberry Scones - Carolyn Williams - https://www.flickr.com/photos/carolynwill/

Chocolate Chip Scones - Kris Arnold - https://www.flickr.com/photos/wka/

CONTENTS

ACKNOWLEDGMENTS

DEDICATION

ABOUT TINA JESSON 2
INTRODUCTION BY TINA 4
A LITTLE BIT OF HISTORY 6
INTRODUCING THE HUMBLE SCONE 7
INTRODUCING CLOTTED CREAM 9
THE GREAT BRITISH DEBATE 10
TINA'S TOP TIPS FOR THE BEST SCONES EVER 12
PLAIN SAVOURY SCONES 14
CHEESE AND ONION SCONES 16
HERBY SAVOURY SCONES 18
MEDITERRANEAN SUN DRIED TOMATO WITH FRESH BASIL & OLIVE SCONES 20
CHEESY SCONES 22
CHEESE & BACON SCONES 24
RAISIN SCONES 26
BLUEBERRY SCONES 28
CHOCOLATE CHIP SCONES 30
WHITE CHOCOLATE CHIP SCONES 32
APPLE & CINNAMON SCONES 34
CRANBERRY SCONES 36
DATE & WALNUT SCONES 38
PUMPKIN SCONES 40
BLACKBERRY & LEMON SCONES 42
TINA'S TRADITIONAL MEMORIES 44
NOTES 56
WHAT'S NEXT FOR TINA'S TRADITIONAL? 66

About The Author
TINA JESSON

Tina Jesson is a Traditional Food Chef & Historian, International Speaker, Writer, Trainer, and native Englander.

Tina has been cooking traditional British cuisine for over 30 years, learning the skill of English farmhouse cooking from 3 generations of family cooks while growing up in England.

She moved to the USA from the Derbyshire region of England when her husband was relocated to Indianapolis with Rolls Royce Aero Engines.

Tina launched Tina's Traditional Old English Kitchen, as a catering company in 2011 which specialised in traditional British food and elegant tea parties, before opening tearooms in various locations across Indiana.

As a trained educator, she continues to give cooking and food preparation classes, classes in British table etiquette, blending workshops and tea tastings and is a sought-after speaker.

Tina can be seen as a regular guest on IndyStyle and Fox59 News and you may have seen her featured in Tea Time Magazine or heard her speak at The World Tea Expo in Las Vegas.

As a published author of "How to Play the Property Game" and "Tina's Traditional Book of..." series which includes such titles as "Tina's Traditional Book of Afternoon Tea, "Tina's Traditional Book of Tea Party Etiquette" and "Tina's Traditional Book of Scones", Tina loves to share her heritage through her writing.

In Tina's Traditional Book of Scones, Tina shares her treasured family scone recipes, that were passed down to her from her great grandmother Gladys Wooley who was born in 1899 and worked as a Scullery Maid at Bradley Hall, Derbyshire, at the time Downton Abbey was set.

The recipes have been updated with Metric and US weights and measures, and rewritten to make them simple to follow, as well as adding some more modern ingredients. So, whether you are a novice or a master baker, you will enjoy this collection of scrumptious scone recipes.

The Building of a British Brand

Between 2011 when Tina first started to develop the Tina's Traditional brand and 2020, she had run tea service at 4 locations in the Indiana area and served over 10,000 guests. One highlight of the business journey was to serve Mrs Pence The Second Lady of the USA, when Mike Pence was governor of Indiana and she has had the privilege to serve at the Governor's Residence on numerous occasions since then.

Tina has supported over 100 charities and community organizations and has made thousands of scones in the process.

Developing a range of jams based on her Grandmothers recipe collection, Tina started with 4 fruit-based varieties adding a further 4 tea-based varieties after speaking at the World Tea Expo in Las Vegas.

Tina was inspired to develop The Tina's Traditional Heritage Range of loose-leaf teas, after working with her master blender & tea merchant, when she had the idea to capture aspects of her mother's fruit garden in the English Fruit Garden blend. There are currently 8 unique blends in the range of over 20 teas available online.

Tina's Traditional Scones Mix was the first bake mix to be developed with her team, and this range grew to include many of the scones, cakes and pastries varieties enjoyed at the tearooms.

During the closedown in March 2020, The Devonshire Cream Tea Care Package was developed to include scones mix, jam, tea and clotted cream and was shipped across the USA to family members and friends who were in lockdown.

"We have to meet people wherever they are at their comfort level, so giving people choices and options has been a really big focus for us." Tina Jesson, Founder of Tina's Traditional

INTRODUCTION BY TINA

Did you know, I built my business on scones?

I first started my business, Tina's Traditional, in 2011, selling scones at farmers markets, selling at 4 markets each week through the hot and hazy summer months and through the snowy cold winters.

And "it's a crummy business" (good scones are so tender and crumbly; the crumbs go everywhere).

I remember an American colleague telling me once that my scones were simply amazing. The best she's ever had. And I remember thinking – "they're JUST SCONES!".

But then in America, scones have such a bad reputation for being dry, hard and tasteless. Thanks Starbucks!

I remember at the farmers market, as people bought them, they would walk off, open the package and eat them on the go – with no clotted cream or jam….Noooooo!

If only I had a tearoom, I could serve them God intended. I could show people how to eat a scone and they would have an experience just like they would if they were in England.

Learning to bake sones was one of the first recipes I ever learnt to bake from my Great Grandma. I even came across the very same 1930's recipe book, which my Grandmother learnt to bake scones from.

So, that's how I ended up building my brand on the humble scone and why scones have such a fond place in my heart and why this "Book of Scones" was my first cookbook. The title was originally published in 2014, just as I opened my tearoom in Carmel Indiana, USA.

In 2020, my publisher suggested I create an updated memories edition, where I've included colour pictures, stories of the experience some of our guests have had at the tearoom, customer comments and mentions of some of charities and community organizations I've had the privilege to work with over the years.

In this book I present a potted history of the humble scone and a brief look back at the beginning of Traditional British Tea Time.

I have prepared my favourite family recipes for both sweet and savoury scones, together with serving suggestions. I've also added a few modern recipes that I have enjoyed making in the English Tea Rooms in Indiana.

How best to use this book:

The recipe layout in this book has been designed to make it easy for you to use in the kitchen and to follow each recipe without lots of page turning.

For me cooking is an art, not a science, and I encourage experimentation. Cooking results can change due to many things, including the ingredients depending on the country you live in, the weather, your oven, and even how hot or cold your hands are.

I've found making notes of what happens and what works best, helps me to duplicate the best results. To help you do the same, I've added special notes sections on each recipe page and at the back, for you to note down what works for you, and what modifications you made.

Measurements are given in Metric, Imperial and US; just pick the one that suits you best.

I'd love to hear from you and welcome your comments and suggestions on my facebook page at: **facebook.com/TinasTraditional** and my website: **TinasTraditional.com**

Tina

A LITTLE BIT OF HISTORY

The Origin of English Afternoon Tea Time

Afternoon tea is a great British tradition, and scones are a classical accompaniment to a traditional afternoon tea.

To this day, afternoon tea is served between 3 and 4 o'clock in Britain. But when did the traditional afternoon tea first begin?

The story has it that it first began to be served as an afternoon meal in the 1700s. Originally it was a meal served to working men to get them through the day between midday and the evening meal. This meal consisted of tea with cooked meats, cheese on thick sliced bread, scones and cakes, it is said to be eaten standing up, hence the expression "high" tea.

English tea time was introduced to the upper classes by the Duchess of Bedford, Anna Maria Russell, in the mid-1840s during a visit to the Duke of Rutland at Belvoir Castle. Right up to this time the gap between the midday meal and the evening dinner had grown to over 7 hours. This new light meal of tea with bread and butter sandwiches and light cakes, was welcomed to fill the long afternoon gap between the two main meals.

The Duchess went on to introduce the practice of inviting acquaintances to afternoon tea to London society, and most importantly to Queen Victoria, her long term friend. It soon became stylish for London society to partake of afternoon tea, and before long a whole industry was built up around afternoon tea, with tea services, tea paraphernalia and eventually public tea rooms.

INTRODUCING THE HUMBLE SCONE

The humble scone is an intrinsic ingredient of a traditional English afternoon tea, usually served with a pot of tea and clotted Devonshire cream. The scone recipe is very similar to a pastry with the basic requirements of flour and baking powder, it can be sweet or savoury and is a very simple recipe that produces tasty results.

History of the Scone

The scone is reputed to have been first invented in Scotland in the 16th century and indeed it is claimed as a national Scottish dish. The original Scottish scone varied significantly from the scones we see today, made as they were from unleavened oats, rolled to the size of a medium plate and baked on a griddle, then cut into "pizza" style triangles.

Today's basic scone recipes include flour, baking powder and butter, which brings it closer to the variety of scones we know today. Indeed today's recipes for the humble scones continue to evolve, including:

- "dropped" or "drop" scones, like a pancake, after the method of dropping the batter onto the griddle or frying pan to cook it,
- lemonade scone, is made with lemonade and cream instead of butter and milk.
- lightly sweetened fruit scones are made with a variety of fruits including berries, cherries, apples, pumpkins, currants, and raisins. Sweetened scones tend to be served with clotted cream and jams.
- savoury scones can offer a hearty meal, with the recipes containing cheese, onion, and bacon

Commercially produced scones, are usually round in shape, or hexagonal for space efficiency. Whereas today's home made, scones come in a variety of shapes and sizes, including circles, squares, rectangles and traditional triangles. Home baked scones are usually made from treasured family recipes, rather than commercial recipe books.

"SCON"? OR "SCONE"?

The word "Scone" was first mentioned in the Oxford English Dictionary in **1513**. Ever since, the debate has raged over whether is it pronounced "scon" or "scone". As the lines of this old poem demonstrate:

> I asked the maid in dulcet tone
>
> To order me a buttered scone
>
> The silly girl has been and gone
>
> And ordered me a buttered scone.

Both pronunciations are correct, and will vary depending on your origin. The "scon" pronunciation is favoured in Scotland and Ireland. While "scone" tends to be the preferred pronunciation for England, the United States, Australia, Canada, and New Zealand.

So whether you prefer to call it a "scon" or a "scone", you'll love these scrumptious family recipes.

INTRODUCING CLOTTED CREAM

Clotted cream is an essential element for serving scones in the traditional way and can be found everywhere in the UK where Afternoon Tea is served.

Clotted cream is served on a scone, with a dollop of raspberry or strawberry jam together with a pot of tea. When served in this way it is known as a Cream Tea.

Clotted cream is a very thick cream with a very high fat content of at least

55% which gives it such a luxurious texture and taste. In comparison single cream has a fat content of only 18%.

The flavour has been described as a "nutty, cooked milk" with a "rich sweet flavour" and a grainy texture.

Of uncertain provenance, clotted cream is primarily now produced in the south west of England in the counties of Cornwall and Devon.

The name "Cornish Clotted Cream" is protected by a European Directive, for which the fat content must be 55% and the milk must originate from Cornwall. Whereas Devonshire Clotted Cream must have a fat content of 55% and originate from Devon.

Double cream: A dense cream skimmed from the surface of milk. With a butterfat content of 48%, it is much more decadent than whipped cream but slightly lower than clotted cream.

In the United States, jars of authentic Devonshire clotted cream and double Devon cream can be found online at **TinasTraditional.com** and can be shipped across the USA

Mock versions can also be made using cream cheese or sour cream or mascarpone, or heavy whipping cream with sugar and vanilla added.

THE GREAT BRITISH DEBATE

Cream First? or Jam First?

The cream tea is traditionally a speciality of the English Counties of Devon and Cornwall. And so, there are two schools of thought in the way clotted cream is applied to your cream tea scone.

The Devonshire Way

Devon is a County in the South West coasts of England. Historically noted for having the oldest bakery in the world, they also claim historical evidence to suggest that the Cream Tea originated in Devon at the Tavistock Benedictine Abbey over 1,000 years ago, when the monks fed their workers a cream tea consisting of bread, clotted cream and strawberry jam.

Traditionally they spread the **cream first** onto the scone, then "dollop" the jam on top. **Served this way it is known as a Devonshire Cream Tea.**

The Cornish Way

The neighbouring county of Cornwall also claim to be the origin of the ancient art of cream tea.

Traditionally they spread the **jam first** onto the scone, then "dollop" the cream on top. **Served this way it is a Cornish Cream Tea.**

This is a contention between many British folks, including my husband. My view is that both are correct, and it becomes a matter of personal choice. Why not try both, to find out which tastes best for you.

Either way, both are of course served with a pot of tea.

What type of tea?

In the USA, black tea is usually referred to as "English Breakfast Tea". While in the UK, the every day "Tea" or "cuppa" that tea drinkers drink is usually just called :

An English cuppa is usually served hot, and with milk, and occassionally a teaspoon of sugar.

TINA'S TOP TIPS
for the best Scones Ever

Use organic butter, flour and free range, farm reared or organic eggs whenever possible.

If you want to make more than 6 scones per batch, then double the recipe

Use non- aluminum baking powder for the best flavor profile.

Before you start, ensure everything is as cool as possible (but not frozen), that includes your ingredients (particularly the butter), your equipment, and your hands.

To get the fluffiest scones, add plenty of air to the flour by sieving at least five times.

When mixing together, do it lightly and quickly. Mixture should be pulled lightly together into a spongy dough. Try not to over rub or over-knead.

Roll the dough gently to a thickness of 1 inch or 2.5cm, do not overwork.

Twisting or stretching the dough when cutting can ruin scones. So when cutting, cut quickly and cleanly with a sharp knife. If using a cutter, push straight down and pull straight up as quickly and cleanly as possible.

Too much egg wash will stop the scones rising. When coating with egg wash, brush off the excess before brushing the scone very lightly.

To prevent sticking use parchment paper, not wax paper, as a liner on your baking sheets. Alternatively use a silicon sheet to save on washing up, just rinse then dry.

To get the best results, place scones in the hottest part of the oven, the top.

Tina's Traditional Book of Scones

PLAIN SAVOURY SCONES

The plain scone is the basic scone recipe, and can be served warm or cold.

SERVING SUGGESTION

Tasty served warm, slice horizontally and sandwich with slices of cheese or use to dip into hot soup. Suitable for freezing.

INGREDIENTS

Makes 6 Scones

Metric/Imperial

225g / 8oz self-raising flour
½ teaspoon salt
50g / 2oz butter
150 ml / ¼ pint full fat milk

US

2 cups all-purpose flour sifted with 2 teaspoons of baking powder
½ teaspoon salt
½ stick butter
½ cup full fat milk

METHOD

Add flour, baking powder and salt to a mixing bowl or food mixer.

Cut butter into slices and add to bowl.

Rub using your fingertips or if using a mixer, turn to number 1 speed, until mixture resembles breadcrumbs.

Stir in enough milk to make a soft dough.

Knead lightly on a floured surface, then roll out to 1cm/½ inch thick.

Use circular 5cm/2 inch cutter, or cut into triangles, or any preferred shapes.

To prevent sticking, dip cutter in flour and put scones on a greased baking sheet or use baking parchment.

Use a little egg or milk to glaze with a pastry brush.

Bake in a hot oven: 450F, 230C, Gas Mark 8; Fan Assisted: 400F, 210C.

Bake for 15 minutes until well risen, golden and cooked.

Recipe Notes:

....

....

....

....

Tina's Traditional Book of Scones

CHEESE & ONION SCONES

The cheese and onion scone makes a tasty and filling snack, and can be served warm or cold.

SERVING SUGGESTION

Tasty served warm, slice horizontally and spread with a layer of green tomato chutney, Branston Pickle or onion relish. Suitable for freezing.

INGREDIENTS
Makes 6 Scones

Metric/Imperial

- 225g / 8oz self-raising flour
- 1 teaspoon of dried English mustard
- ½ teaspoon salt
- 50g / 2oz butter
- 50g / 2oz grated strong cheddar cheese
- ½ large or 1 small white onion grated
- 150 ml / ¼ pint full fat milk

US

- 2 cups all-purpose flour sifted with 2 teaspoons of baking powder
- 1 teaspoon of dried English mustard
- ½ teaspoon salt
- ½ stick butter
- ¼ cup grated strong cheddar cheese
- ¼ large or 1 small white onion grated
- ½ cup full fat mil

METHOD

Add flour, baking powder, mustard power and salt to a mixing bowl or food mixer.

Cut butter into slices and add to bowl.

Rub using your fingertips or if using a mixer, turn to number 1 speed, until mixture resembles breadcrumbs.

Add grated cheese and grated onion.

Stir in enough milk to make a soft dough. You may need to use less milk as the onion provides some moisture.

Knead lightly on a floured surface then roll out to 1cm/½ inch thick.

Cut scones using a 5cm/2 inch cutter.

To prevent sticking, dip cutter in flour and put cut scones on a greased baking sheet or use baking parchment.

Use a little egg or milk to glaze with a pastry brush.

Bake in a hot oven: 450F, 230C, Gas Mark 8; Fan Assisted: 400F, 210C.

Bake for 15 minutes until well risen, golden and cooked.

Recipe Notes:

Tina's Traditional Book of Scones

HERBY SAVOURY SCONES

**Another tasty savoury snack,
which can be served warm or cold.**

SERVING SUGGESTION

Tasty served warm, slice horizontally and spread with a thick layer of cream cheese or soft goat's cheese, a chunk of cheddar and tomato. . Suitable for freezing.

INGREDIENTS
Makes 6 Scones

Metric/Imperial	US
225g / 8oz self-raising flour	2 cups all-purpose flour sifted with 2 teaspoons of baking powder
½ teaspoon salt	½ teaspoon salt
1 teaspoon of single or mixed herbs (finely chopped fresh or dried) try Rosemary, Thyme, Dill	1 teaspoon of single or mixed herbs (finely chopped fresh or dried) try Rosemary, Thyme, Dill
50g / 2oz butter	½ stick butter
150 ml / ¼ pint full fat milk	½ cup full fat milk

METHOD

Add flour, baking powder, herbs and salt to a mixing bowl or food mixer.

Cut butter into slices and add to bowl.

Rub using your fingertips or if using a mixer, turn to number 1 speed, until mixture resembles breadcrumbs.

Stir in enough milk to make a soft dough.

Knead lightly on a floured surface then roll out to 1cm/½ inch thick.

Cut scones using a 5cm/2 inch cutter.

To prevent sticking, dip cutter in flour and put cut scones on a greased baking sheet or use baking parchment.

Use a little egg or milk to glaze with a pastry brush.

Bake in a hot oven: 450F, 230C, Gas Mark 8; Fan Assisted: 400F, 210C.

Bake for 15 minutes until well risen, golden and cooked.

Recipe Notes:

Tina's Traditional Book of Scones

MEDITERRANEAN SUN DRIED TOMATO WITH FRESH BASIL & OLIVE SCONES

Another tasty savoury snack, which can be served warm or cold.

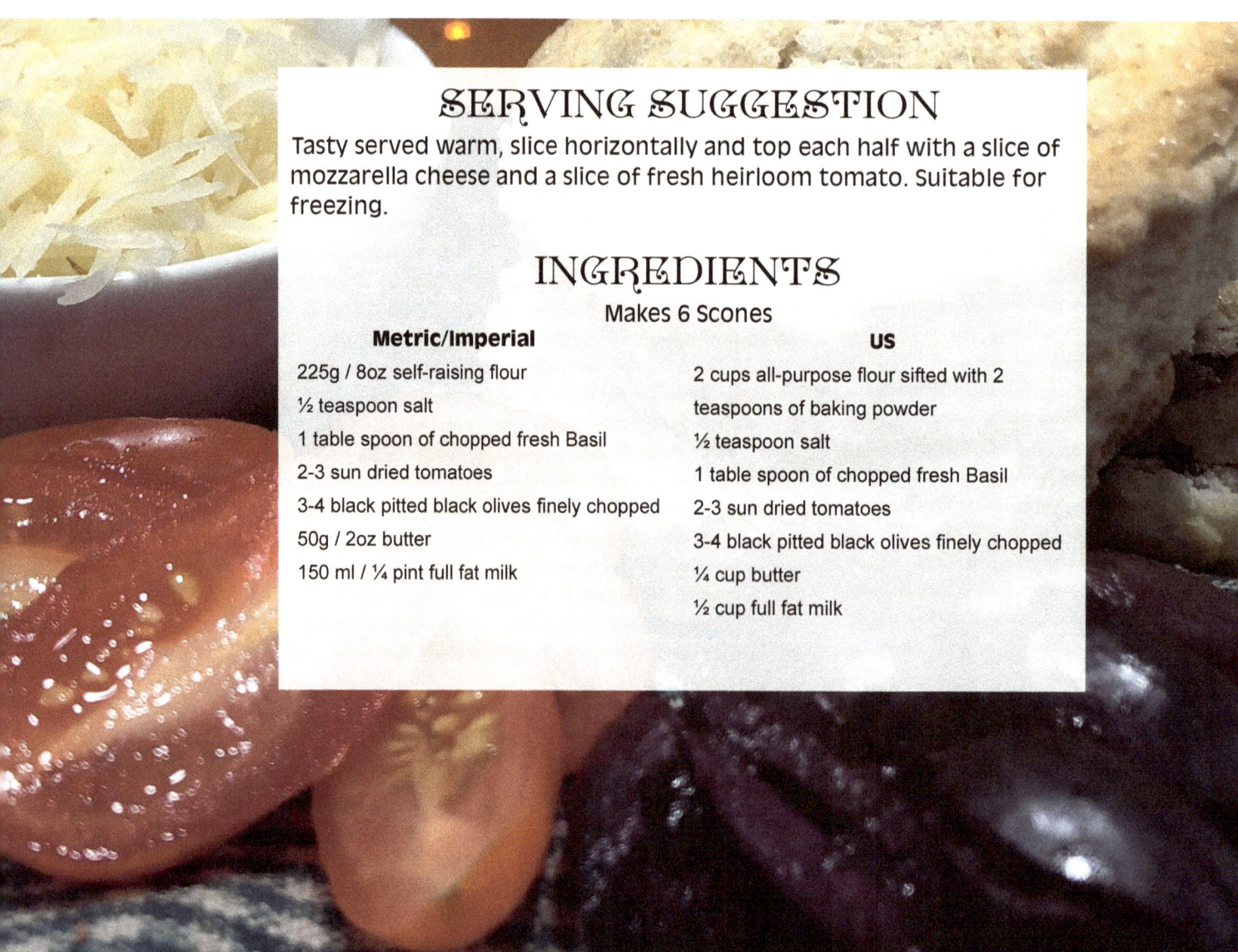

SERVING SUGGESTION

Tasty served warm, slice horizontally and top each half with a slice of mozzarella cheese and a slice of fresh heirloom tomato. Suitable for freezing.

INGREDIENTS
Makes 6 Scones

Metric/Imperial	US
225g / 8oz self-raising flour	2 cups all-purpose flour sifted with 2 teaspoons of baking powder
½ teaspoon salt	½ teaspoon salt
1 table spoon of chopped fresh Basil	1 table spoon of chopped fresh Basil
2-3 sun dried tomatoes	2-3 sun dried tomatoes
3-4 black pitted black olives finely chopped	3-4 black pitted black olives finely chopped
50g / 2oz butter	¼ cup butter
150 ml / ¼ pint full fat milk	½ cup full fat milk

METHOD

Add flour, baking powder, herbs and salt to a mixing bowl or food mixer.

Cut butter into slices and add to bowl.

Rub using your fingertips or if using a mixer, turn to number 1 speed, until mixture resembles breadcrumbs.

Stir in basil, tomatoes and olives.

Stir in enough milk to make a soft dough.

Knead lightly on a floured surface then roll out to 1cm/½ inch thick.

Cut scones using a 5cm/2 inch cutter.

To prevent sticking, dip cutter in flour and put cut scones on a greased baking sheet or use baking parchment.

Use a little egg or milk to glaze with a pastry brush.

Bake in a hot oven: 450F, 230C, Gas Mark 8; Fan Assisted: 400F, 210C.

Bake for 15 minutes until well risen, golden and cooked.

Recipe Notes:

CHEESY SCONES

**Another tasty savoury snack,
which can be served warm or cold.**

SERVING SUGGESTION

Tasty served warm, slice horizontally and spread with thick layer of cream cheese or soft goat's cheese, or use whole to dip in a hot soup. Alternatively make a sandwich scone with ham & tomato. Suitable for freezing.

INGREDIENTS

Makes 6 Scones

Metric/Imperial

225g / 8oz self-raising flour

½ teaspoon salt

50g / 2oz grated cheese plus extra for topping

50g / 2oz butter

150 ml / ¼ pint full fat milk

US

2 cups all-purpose flour sifted with 2 teaspoons of baking powder

½ teaspoon salt

½ cup grated cheese plus extra for topping

½ stick butter

½ cup full fat milk

METHOD

Add flour, baking powder, and salt to a mixing bowl or food mixer.

Cut butter into slices and add to bowl.

Rub using your fingertips or if using a mixer, turn to number 1 speed, until mixture resembles breadcrumbs.

Add grated cheese.

Stir in enough milk to make a soft dough.

Knead lightly on a floured surface then roll out to 1cm/½ inch thick.

Cut scones using a 5cm/2 inch cutter.

To prevent sticking, dip cutter in flour and put cut scones on a greased baking sheet or use baking parchment.

Use a little egg or milk to glaze with a pastry brush.

Sprinkle each scone with a little extra grated cheese.

Bake in a hot oven: 450F, 230C, Gas Mark 8; Fan Assisted: 400F, 210C.

Bake for 15 minutes until well risen, golden and cooked.

Recipe Notes:

CHEESE & BACON SCONES

**Mouth watering, tasty and filling,
can be served warm or cold.**

SERVING SUGGESTION

Tasty served warm, slice horizontally and make a sandwich of cheddar cheese and Branston Pickle or spread with thick layer of cream cheese or soft goat's cheese, or use whole to dip in a hot soup. Suitable for freezing.

INGREDIENTS

Makes 6 Scones

Metric/Imperial

- 225g / 8oz self-raising flour
- ½ teaspoon salt
- 50g / 2oz grated cheese plus extra for topping
- 50g / 2oz finely chopped cooked bacon
- 50g / 2oz butter
- 150 ml / ¼ pint full fat milk

US

- 2 cups all-purpose flour sifted with 2 teaspoons of baking powder
- ½ teaspoon salt
- ¼ cup grated cheese plus extra for topping
- ¼ cup of finely chopped cooked bacon
- ½ stick butter
- ½ cup full fat milk

METHOD

Add flour, baking powder, and salt to a mixing bowl or food mixer.

Cut butter into slices and add to bowl.

Rub using your fingertips or if using a mixer, turn to number 1 speed, until mixture resembles breadcrumbs.

Add grated cheese and chopped bacon.

Stir in enough milk to make a soft dough.

Knead lightly on a floured surface then roll out to 1cm/½ inch thick.

Cut scones using a 5cm/2 inch cutter.

To prevent sticking, dip cutter in flour and put cut scones on a greased baking sheet or use baking parchment.

Use a little egg or milk to glaze with a pastry brush.

Sprinkle each scone with a little extra grated cheese.

Bake in a hot oven: 450F, 230C, Gas Mark 8; Fan Assisted: 400F, 210C.

Bake for 15 minutes until well risen, golden and cooked.

Recipe Notes:

RAISIN SCONES

A quick and tasty sweet raisin snack, which can be served warm or cold.

SERVING SUGGESTION

Tasty served warm, slice horizontally serve open faced with clotted cream and fruit jam or lemon curd. Suitable for freezing.

INGREDIENTS

Makes 6 Scones

Metric/Imperial	US
225g / 8oz self-raising flour	2 cups all-purpose flour sifted with 2 teaspoons of baking powder
½ teaspoon salt	½ teaspoon salt
2oz sugar	2oz sugar
50g / 2oz raisins	¼ cup raisins
50g / 2oz butter	½ stick butter
150 ml / ¼ pint full fat milk	½ cup full fat milk

METHOD

Add flour, baking powder and salt to a mixing bowl or food mixer.

Cut butter into slices and add to bowl.

Rub using your fingertips or if using a mixer, turn to number 1 speed, until mixture resembles breadcrumbs.

Add sugar and mix.

Add raisins.

Stir in enough milk to make a soft dough.

Knead lightly on a floured surface then roll out to 1cm/½ inch thick.

Cut scones using a 5cm/2 inch cutter.

To prevent sticking, dip cutter in flour and put cut scones on a greased baking sheet or use baking parchment.

Use a little egg or milk to glaze with a pastry brush.

Bake in a hot oven: 450F, 230C, Gas Mark 8; Fan Assisted: 400F, 210C.

Bake for 15 minutes until well risen, golden and cooked.

Recipe Notes:

Tina's Traditional Book of Scones

BLUEBERRY SCONES

A quick and tasty sweet snack, which can be served warm or cold.

SERVING SUGGESTION

Tasty served warm, slice horizontally serve open faced with clotted cream and fruit jam or lemon curd. Suitable for freezing.

INGREDIENTS

Makes 6 Scones

Metric/Imperial	US
225g / 8oz self-raising flour	2 cups all-purpose flour sifted with 2 teaspoons of baking powder
½ teaspoon salt	½ teaspoon salt
2oz sugar	2oz sugar
50g / 2oz fresh or frozen blueberries	¼ cup fresh or frozen blueberries
50g / 2oz butter	½ stick butter
150 ml / ¼ pint full fat milk	½ cup full fat milk

METHOD

Add flour baking powder and salt to a mixing bowl or food mixer.

Cut butter into slices and add to bowl.

Rub using your fingertips or if using a mixer, turn to number 1 speed, until mixture resembles breadcrumbs.

Add sugar and mix.

Stir in enough milk to make a soft dough.

Add Fresh or frozen blueberries and mix carefully by hand so not to burst the fruit.

Knead lightly on a floured surface then roll out to 1cm/½ inch thick.

Cut scones using a 5cm/2 inch cutter.

To prevent sticking, dip cutter in flour and put cut scones on a greased baking sheet or use baking parchment.

Use a little egg or milk to glaze with a pastry brush.

Bake in a hot oven: 450F, 230C, Gas Mark 8; Fan Assisted: 400F, 210C.

Bake for 15 minutes until well risen, golden and cooked.

Recipe Notes:

CHOCOLATE CHIP SCONES

A chocolaty snack, which can be served warm or cold.

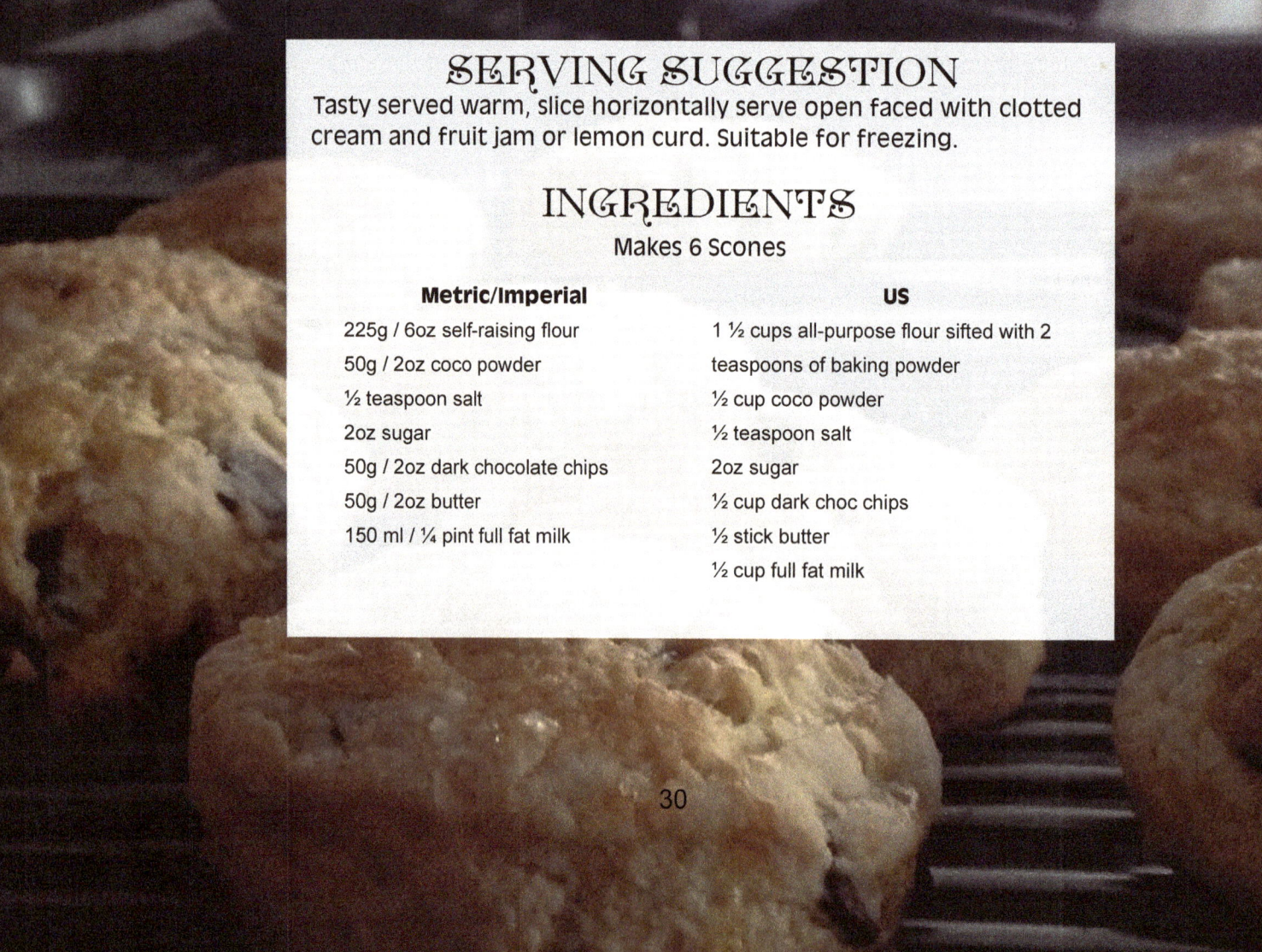

SERVING SUGGESTION

Tasty served warm, slice horizontally serve open faced with clotted cream and fruit jam or lemon curd. Suitable for freezing.

INGREDIENTS

Makes 6 Scones

Metric/Imperial	US
225g / 6oz self-raising flour	1 ½ cups all-purpose flour sifted with 2 teaspoons of baking powder
50g / 2oz coco powder	½ cup coco powder
½ teaspoon salt	½ teaspoon salt
2oz sugar	2oz sugar
50g / 2oz dark chocolate chips	½ cup dark choc chips
50g / 2oz butter	½ stick butter
150 ml / ¼ pint full fat milk	½ cup full fat milk

METHOD

Add flour, baking powder, coco powder and salt to a mixing bowl or food mixer.

Cut butter into slices and add to bowl.

Rub using your fingertips or if using a mixer, turn to number 1 speed, until mixture resembles breadcrumbs.

Add sugar and mix.

Stir in enough milk to make a soft dough.

Add chocolate chips and knead by hand to mix in.

Knead lightly on a floured surface then roll out to 1cm/½ inch thick.

Cut scones using a 5cm/2 inch cutter.

To prevent sticking, dip cutter in flour and put cut scones on a greased baking sheet or use baking parchment.

Use a little egg or milk to glaze with a pastry brush.

Bake in a hot oven: 450F, 230C, Gas Mark 8; Fan Assisted: 400F, 210C.

Bake for 15 minutes until well risen, golden and cooked,

Recipe Notes:

WHITE CHOCOLATE CHIP SCONES

A chocolaty snack, which can be served warm or cold.

SERVING SUGGESTION

Tasty served warm, slice horizontally serve open faced with clotted cream and fruit jam or lemon curd. Suitable for freezing.

INGREDIENTS

Makes 6 Scones

Metric/Imperial	US
225g / 8oz self-raising flour	2 cups all-purpose flour sifted with 2 teaspoons of baking powder
½ teaspoon salt	½ teaspoon salt
2oz sugar	2oz sugar
50g / 2oz white chocolate chips	½ cup White choc chips
50g / 2oz butter	½ stick cup butter
150 ml / ¼ pint full fat milk	½ cup full fat milk

METHOD

Add flour, baking powder and salt to a mixing bowl or food mixer.

Cut butter into slices and add to bowl.

Rub using your fingertips or if using a mixer, turn to number 1 speed, until mixture resembles breadcrumbs.

Add sugar and mix.

Stir in enough milk to make a soft dough.

Add White chocolate chips and knead by hand to mix in.

Knead lightly on a floured surface then roll out to 1cm/½ inch thick.

Cut scones using a 5cm/2 inch cutter.

To prevent sticking, dip cutter in flour and put cut scones on a greased baking sheet or use baking parchment.

Use a little egg or milk to glaze with a pastry brush.

Bake in a hot oven: 450F, 230C, Gas Mark 8; Fan Assisted: 400F, 210C.

Bake for 15 minutes until well risen, golden and cooked.

Recipe Notes:

Tina's Traditional Book of Scones

APPLE & CINNAMON SCONES

A scrumptious, tasty and filling treat, which can be served warm or cold.

SERVING SUGGESTION

Tasty served warm, slice horizontally serve open faced with clotted cream and fruit jam or lemon curd. Suitable for freezing.

INGREDIENTS

Makes 6 Scones

Metric/Imperial	US
225g / 8oz self-raising flour	2 cups all-purpose flour sifted with 2 teaspoons of baking powder
½ teaspoon salt	½ teaspoon salt
2oz sugar	2oz sugar
½ teaspoon cinnamon	½ teaspoon cinnamon
50g / 2oz apple grated	¼ cup apple grated
50g / 2oz butter	½ stick butter
150 ml / ¼ pint full fat milk	½ cup full fat milk

METHOD

Add flour, baking powder, cinnamon and salt to a mixing bowl or food mixer.

Cut butter into slices and add to bowl.

Rub using your fingertips or if using a mixer, turn to number 1 speed, until mixture resembles breadcrumbs.

Add sugar and mix.

Add grated apple.

Stir in enough milk to make a soft dough.

Knead lightly on a floured surface then roll out to 1cm/½ inch thick.

Cut scones using a 5cm/2 inch cutter.

To prevent sticking, dip cutter in flour and put cut scones on a greased baking sheet or use baking parchment.

Use a little egg or milk to glaze with a pastry brush.

Bake in a hot oven: 450F, 230C, Gas Mark 8; Fan Assisted: 400F, 210C.

Bake for 15 minutes until well risen, golden and cooked.

Recipe Notes:

Tina's Traditional Book of Scones

CRANBERRY SCONES

A colourful and tasty treat for the festive season, which can be made throughout the year, served warm or cold.

SERVING SUGGESTION

Tasty served warm, slice horizontally serve open faced cream cheese or brie or butter. Suitable for freezing.

INGREDIENTS

Makes 6 Scones

Metric/Imperial

225g / 8oz self-raising flour

½ teaspoon salt

2oz sugar

50g / 2oz dried cranberries

50g / 2oz butter

150 ml / ¼ pint full fat milk

US

2 cups all-purpose flour sifted with 2 teaspoons of baking powder

½ teaspoon salt

2oz sugar

¼ cup dried cranberries

½ stick butter

½ cup full fat milk

METHOD

Add flour, baking powder and salt to a mixing bowl or food mixer.

Cut butter into slices and add to bowl.

Rub using your fingertips or if using a mixer, turn to number 1 speed, until mixture resembles breadcrumbs.

Add sugar and mix.

Stir in enough milk to make a soft dough.

Add dried cranberries and knead by hand to mix in.

Knead lightly on a floured surface then roll out to 1cm/½ inch thick.

Cut scones using a 5cm/2 inch cutter.

To prevent sticking, dip cutter in flour and put cut scones on a greased baking sheet or use baking parchment.

Use a little egg or milk to glaze with a pastry brush.

Bake in a hot oven: 450F, 230C, Gas Mark 8; Fan Assisted: 400F, 210C.

Bake for 15 minutes until well risen, golden and cooked.

Recipe Notes:

DATE & WALNUT SCONES

A tasty sweet snack, which can be served warm or cold.

SERVING SUGGESTION

Tasty served warm, slice horizontally serve open faced with cream cheese, brie or goats cheese. Suitable for freezing.

INGREDIENTS

Makes 6 Scones

Metric/Imperial	US
225g / 8oz self-raising flour	2 cups all-purpose flour sifted with 2 teaspoons of baking powder
½ teaspoon salt	½ teaspoon salt
2oz sugar	2oz sugar
25g / 1oz chopped dried dates	¼ cup chopped dried dates
25g / 1oz chopped walnuts	¼ cup chopped walnuts
50g / 2oz butter	½ stick butter
150 ml / ¼ pint full fat milk	½ cup full fat milk

METHOD

Add flour, baking powder and salt to a mixing bowl or food mixer.

Cut butter into slices and add to bowl.

Rub using your fingertips or if using a mixer, turn to number 1 speed, until mixture resembles breadcrumbs.

Add sugar and mix.

Stir in enough milk to make a soft dough.

Add chopped dates and walnuts. Knead by hand to mix in.

Knead lightly on a floured surface then roll out to 1cm/½ inch thick.

Cut scones using a 5cm/2 inch cutter.

To prevent sticking, dip cutter in flour and put cut scones on a greased baking sheet or use baking parchment.

Use a little egg or milk to glaze with a pastry brush.

Bake in a hot oven: 450F, 230C, Gas Mark 8; Fan Assisted: 400F, 210C.

Bake for 15 minutes until well risen, golden and cooked.

Recipe Notes:

PUMPKIN SCONES

A tasty seasonal treat, which can be served warm or cold.

SERVING SUGGESTION

Tasty served warm, slice horizontally serve open faced with butter. Suitable for freezing.

INGREDIENTS

Makes 6 Scones

Metric/Imperial	US
225g / 8oz self-raising flour	2 cups all-purpose flour sifted with 2 teaspoons of baking powder
½ teaspoon salt	½ teaspoon salt
2oz sugar	2oz sugar
50g / 2oz pumpkin mix or fresh pumpkin	½ cup pumpkin mix or fresh pumpkin
50g / 2oz butter	½ cup butter
150 ml / ¼ pint full fat milk	½ cup full fat milk

METHOD

Add flour, baking powder and salt to a mixing bowl or food mixer.

Cut butter into slices and add to bowl.

Rub using your fingertips or if using a mixer, turn to number 1 speed, until mixture resembles breadcrumbs.

Peel, seed and coarsely chop butternut pumpkin and steam for **10 minutes** or until very soft. Mash pumpkin to a rough puree. Add ½ teaspoon of Cinnamon. Let cool.

Add sugar and mix. Add pumpkin mix to scone mix and mix in.

Add enough milk to make a soft dough.

Knead lightly on a floured surface then roll out to 1cm/½ inch thick.

Cut scones using a 5cm/2 inch cutter.

To prevent sticking, dip cutter in flour and put cut scones on a greased baking sheet or use baking parchment.

Use a little egg or milk to glaze with a pastry brush.

Bake in a hot oven: 450F, 230C, Gas Mark 8; Fan Assisted: 400F, 210C.

Bake for **15 minutes** until well risen, golden and cooked.

Recipe Notes:

BLACKBERRY & LEMON SCONES

A comforting sweet treat, which can be served warm or cold.

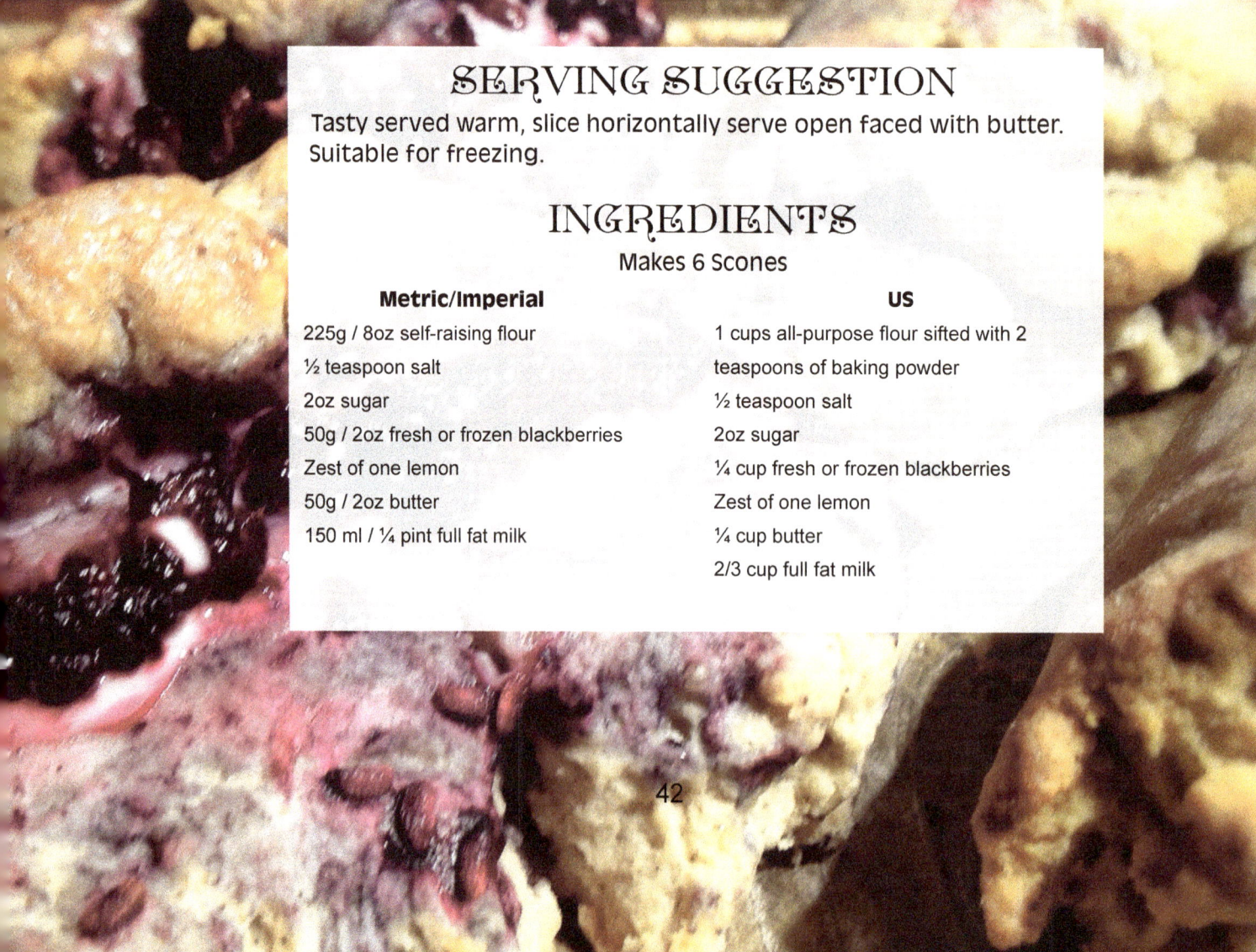

SERVING SUGGESTION

Tasty served warm, slice horizontally serve open faced with butter. Suitable for freezing.

INGREDIENTS
Makes 6 Scones

Metric/Imperial	US
225g / 8oz self-raising flour	1 cups all-purpose flour sifted with 2 teaspoons of baking powder
½ teaspoon salt	½ teaspoon salt
2oz sugar	2oz sugar
50g / 2oz fresh or frozen blackberries	¼ cup fresh or frozen blackberries
Zest of one lemon	Zest of one lemon
50g / 2oz butter	¼ cup butter
150 ml / ¼ pint full fat milk	2/3 cup full fat milk

METHOD

Add flour, baking powder and salt to a mixing bowl or food mixer.

Cut butter into slices and add to bowl.

Rub using your fingertips or if using a mixer, turn to number 1 speed, until mixture resembles breadcrumbs.

Add sugar and mix.

Add lemon zest and blackberries. Carefully mix in to avoid crushing the fruit

Add enough milk to make a soft dough.

Knead lightly on a floured surface then roll out to 1cm/½ inch thick.

Cut scones using a 5cm/2 inch cutter.

To prevent sticking, dip cutter in flour and put cut scones on a greased baking sheet or use baking parchment.

Use a little egg or milk to glaze with a pastry brush.

Bake in a hot oven: 450F, 230C, Gas Mark 8; Fan Assisted: 400F, 210C.

Bake for 15 minutes until well risen, golden and cooked.

Recipe Notes:

Tina's Traditional MEMORIES

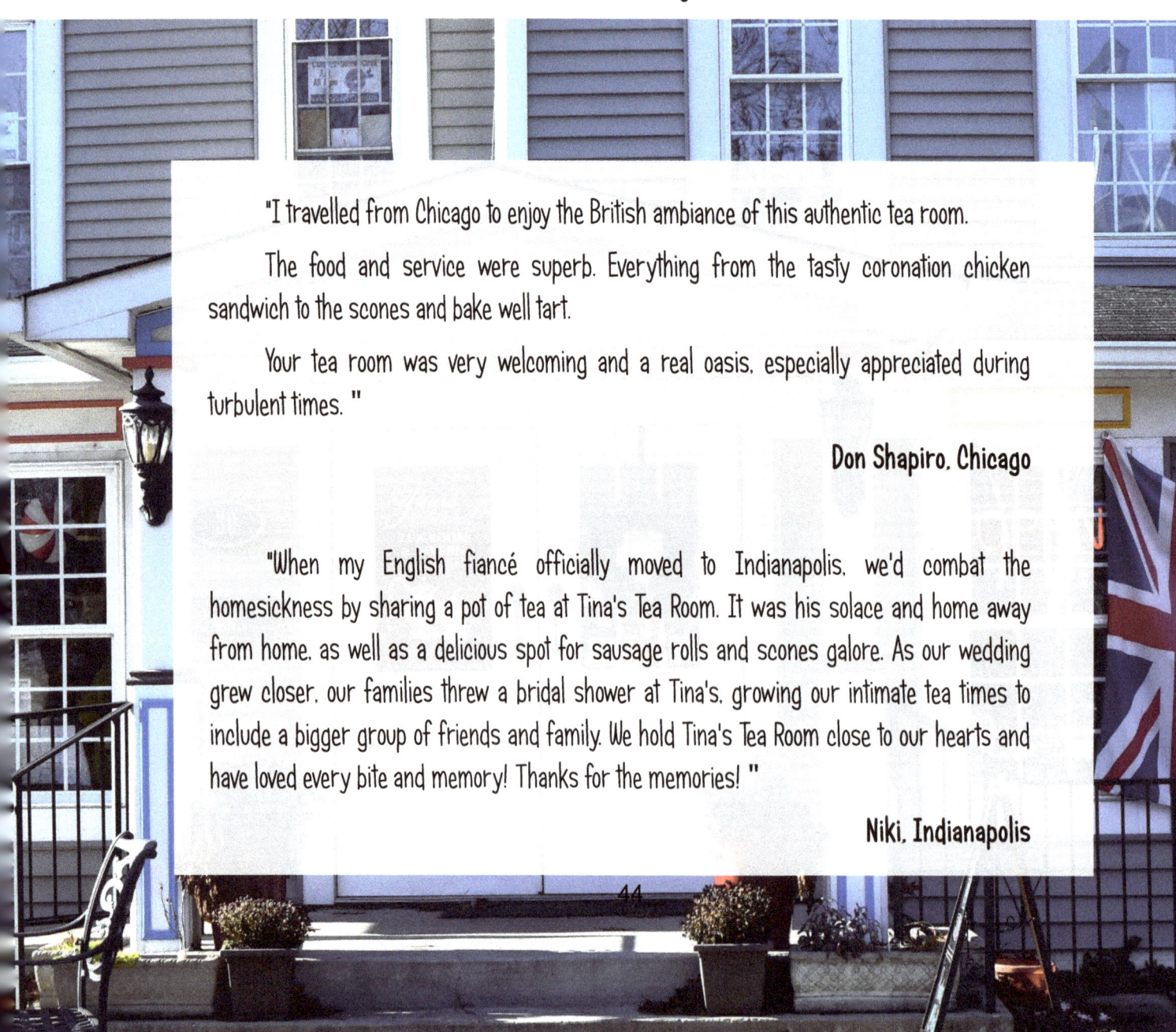

"I travelled from Chicago to enjoy the British ambiance of this authentic tea room.

The food and service were superb. Everything from the tasty coronation chicken sandwich to the scones and bake well tart.

Your tea room was very welcoming and a real oasis, especially appreciated during turbulent times."

Don Shapiro, Chicago

"When my English fiancé officially moved to Indianapolis, we'd combat the homesickness by sharing a pot of tea at Tina's Tea Room. It was his solace and home away from home, as well as a delicious spot for sausage rolls and scones galore. As our wedding grew closer, our families threw a bridal shower at Tina's, growing our intimate tea times to include a bigger group of friends and family. We hold Tina's Tea Room close to our hearts and have loved every bite and memory! Thanks for the memories!"

Niki, Indianapolis

Tina's Traditional Book of Scones

Tina's Traditional MEMORIES

I found Tina's Traditional Tearoom after I had a wonderful High Tea experience at the luxurious West Baden Springs hotel a few years ago. I wanted to see if there was anything local and was ecstatic to find one so close to where I live. My first reservation went to someone I love and cherish very much, my grandmother.

After a long and arduous medical journey, my grandparents moved from their home of 50+ years to be closer to family in Indiana. When they moved, it was around my grandmother's birthday and I wanted her to have a magnificent experience since having to move so suddenly can be overwhelming. I reserved two High Tea experiences for my grandmother and invited my mother to go with her so they could have a Mother-Daughter birthday.

What made this so much more memorable was that, due to the medical struggles, my grandmother was wheelchair bound and was hesitant to go. When I called Tina's, I asked a lot of questions about accessibility and comfort since my grandmother was mostly recovered but still had some mobility issues. Not only was the manager accommodating but they provided extra details to make my grandmother as comfortable as possible.

It seems like such a small thing but it meant the world in a time of great change. My grandmother was starstruck by the experience and continued to talk about it for months afterward. As a thank you, she gave me a bag of the 1776 blend, which I have been happily purchasing for months now whenever I run out.

Since then, I have sent my parents to a Dinner with Mr. Darcey event (which they dressed up for) and the aforementioned high tea experience I had with a friend.

Though the physical doors may be closing to the tea room, so long as the virtual ones are open, Tina's legacy will continue to thrive and grow within the community it created....and, as long as the 1776 blend continues to sell, I will be right alongside it, smiling at the memories and wishing the best for the future with every cupful I continue to make. Once again, thank you for all that you have done to build this community and I look forward to seeing where the future takes you."

Molly Harris

47

Tina's Traditional Book of Scones

Tina's Traditional MEMORIES

That last year my granddaughter Lily and I went to Tina's Traditional Tea Room in Indy. Lily was delighted with everything there and as we had tea, we pretended we were very fancy ladies.

We spoke with English accents and Lily was fascinated with the Queen. We talked about visiting England together some day and Lily decided that I could paint a china cup for the Queen and we would go to England to deliver it for her birthday. She kind of had the idea that we could just go there, walk up to the castle and say, " Hi! It's Lily and Gammaw. We are here to visit the Queen." And we would be invited in for tea and give her the painted tea cup.

Well we didn't get to visit the Queen, but we had the next best thing with high tea at Tina's Traditional tea room. A wonderful day for us. We still talk about it, and about having tea with the Queen! Who knows? It might happen! Unfortunately, due to the Covid , Tina's had to close which just hurt my heart.

Luckily, Tina is still with us. With her Zoom classes teaching how to bake English goodies. I got the dry ingredients sent to me plus two of the correct baking pans! So it is totally great!

Just tonight I attended a Zoom class on baking a Victoria Sponge cake with a raspberry filling and I LOVED it. I immediately signed up for the scone class and am looking forward to many more classes. Tina is excellent at explaining the little nuances that make all the difference. Thank you so much for continuing the English Tea Tradition in Indianapolis, even though you don't have to live in Indiana to do the class!

Stay safe and eat more cake!!

Joyce Dwulet

Tina's Traditional MEMORIES

> Our women's group visited Tina's Tea room. We had such a sonderful time! The food and tea were delicious. You and your staff were very attentive to our table and we appreciated it.

> Thank you for lavishing me with your kindness. I loved the lunch. very special tea. an deven more. hearing your heart.

> Special thanks to you for making our wedding shower so very beautiful! Everyone appreicated everythign you and your staff did to make it so nice. We had every little special touch possible and we cannot than you enough!

> What a wonder you are. To share with you, your country, is truly a highligh of this much-travelled gypsy. It was truly an honor to be on this trip.

> Thank you for a lovely and delicious tea. We had a wonderful experience at your charming tea room yesterday.

> My spcial birthday party was so wonderful. Thank you for all you did to make everyone enjoy it

> My daughter and I had such a nice lunch, the food, the tea, and the cakes were all wonderful. Our waiter was very kind and charming.

Tina's Traditional MEMORIES

Tina's Traditional MEMORIES

Best Tea Rooms
PLACES TO WATCH THE ROYAL WEDDING
DELISH.COM

TINA'S TRADITIONAL OLD ENGLISH KITCHEN, CARMEL

visit hamilton county indiana

NOTES

NOTES

Tina's Traditional Book of Scones

NOTES

Tina's Traditional Book of Scones

NOTES

NOTES

What's Next for
TINA'S TRADITIONAL?

How Tina Pivoted the business

We have pivoted our business to be online, selling Tina's Traditional range of teas, jams and bake mixes and teatime accessories via the website where you can have us ship across the USA. Items are also available via Market Wagon, for baked items which can be delivered direct to your door twice per week, for those living in the Central Indiana region. My manager, Heather, will be providing catering direct to homes, as many people feel safer having small gatherings there.

What happened

As you can imagine, the costs for a restaurant space in Carmel is so expensive, especially when we dropped from our original number of 20 plus tables down to just 6 inside, as we complied with social distancing rules.

What's next for Tina

I will be running virtual bake classes each week from my home kitchen, developing more learning programs, creating more amazing experiences, and writing more. I will eventually go to visit the UK where my grownup children both live.

Thank You

You have been so supportive of Tina's Traditional since I started the business in 2011, when I was selling scones at farmers markets. As the brand continues to develop online and as we reach more people across the USA, I think the virtual baking classes are needed now more than ever and sharing my family British recipes is still very dear to my heart.

Tina's Traditional
BAKE ALONG

"Baking the old-fashioned way in a totally new world"

I learnt the art of farmhouse cooking and baking from my Mom, Gran and Great Gran. I discovered one of Grandmas first recipe books dating back from the early 1930's. In it was this...

"Teach your daughters how to bake at home."

"Teach your girls how to bake and cook. Let them take pride in making Scones and Cakes for daddy's tea. Every moment you devote to this most important task will be repaid to you a hundredfold, in both the actual help you will receive in later years and in the pleasure and satisfaction you will derive from knowing that you helped them to become useful and economical housewives themselves."

We use many of my families recipes at Tina's Traditional, including jams, preserves and Grandma's Green Tomato Chutney." I can't eat a cheese sandwich without it". Try it on a 'Toasty' - a grilled cheese made with English cheddar and house made Grandmas green tomato chutney. It really is yummy!

Want to learn how to make scones from Grandmas recipe?

Then check out the next Tina's Traditional Xperience virtual baking class and create a memory for your loved ones or as a team building experience.

Baking Kits included

Enjoy from the comfort of your own home as Tina invites you into her home kitchen, virtually of course.

Check out the next virtual bake class & enjoy with friends.

TinasTraditional.com/special-events

Tina's Traditional TOURS

Join Tina on a visit to the UK

Tina often talks about her life back in the UK. Some of her favorite places, those where she grew up and those which have inspired her, and lets not forget about the food. Amazing grass fed beef and lamb. Artisan breads and cheese, fresh cream and scones .... yummmmm.

Tina asks "would you like to come with me and see for yourself?" and invites you to come along with her on a small group private tour.

Each year she heads of for her England/Derbyshire Tour and The Lowlands of Scotland Tour.

Like the idea of living like a local, with a British born guide as your host, as you visit some of the most amazing places the UK has to offer. You'll have VIP access to a number of unique experiences, crafted personally by Tina.

Sounds like something you'd love to do, then check out her previous tours so you'll be one of the first to get the details of Tina's next visit.

TinasTraditional.com/tours

Tina's Traditional Book of Scones

Tina's Traditional
TEA ROOM SECRETS

"Imagine, its 1988 and the songs in the charts in the UK include, Kylie Minogue's – I should be so Lucky.

I step in to a tearoom in Harrogate, North Yorkshire; hear piano music; it's a Sunday morning; there are clouds in the sky but its relatively sunny; I have my first taste of smoked Scottish salmon with soft creamy scrambled eggs; I even remember what I was wearing; and I think to myself, I'd love to own a business like this tearoom one day – by the time I'm 50…

that was 30 years ago. 30 YEARS AGO! and I still remember the day, how it made me feel and exactly what I ate…that's the most amazing thing about being a tearoom owner – we get to create memories which last a life time. I never dreamed I would be doing it here in the States. And yes, I feel very Lucky!"

This was the opening to one of the sessions at the World Tea Expo in Las Vegas in June 2018, when Tina, shared her pivotal story.

Tina has seen many tearooms, cafes and bakeries close over the years due to owner's illness, burnout and not having the right skills to delegate, generate multiple revenue streams or pivot their business and it's such a shame.

She wants to make sure that others don't make the same mistakes she has made (and she will openly admit she has made many), and share the insider secrets that made her business go from survive to thrive.

Over the years, Tina has developed a number of training programs on business growth & development and now is helping other tea business owners.

If you own a tea business, have a cafe or tea shop (or plan to) you can download the Tina's Traditional business plan and equipment list to help you get started or get further information about Tina's training programs by contacting Tina at:

TheXperienceAcademy.com

THE XPERIENCE ACADEMY
TheXperienceAcademy.com

Also available
MY TRADITIONAL RECIPE JOURNAL

Traditional recipe journal and organiser to collect and organise your favourite family recipe secrets.

A fine companion journal to Tina's Traditional Book of Scones, where you can collect and organise your favourite family recipe secrets.

You can organise your recipes with a custom index, rate your recipe difficulty, record preparation, cooking times and how many the recipe serves. Complete with comprehensive kitchen conversion charts for weights, measures and temperatures.

Generous double page layout for each recipe, to accommodate long ingredient lists and instructions. Copious notes section for you to record sourcing of those important ingredients, and special notes about your recipes.

Excellent family recipe journal, sized to fit your kitchen, with a high quality hardback cover made to last, so you can treasure your personal recipe collection for years to come.

AVAILABLE FROM

LionessPublishing.com/my-traditional-recipe-journal

PUBLISH YOUR FAMILY RECIPES

Publishing your family recipe secrets will preserve your treasured recipes through the generations.

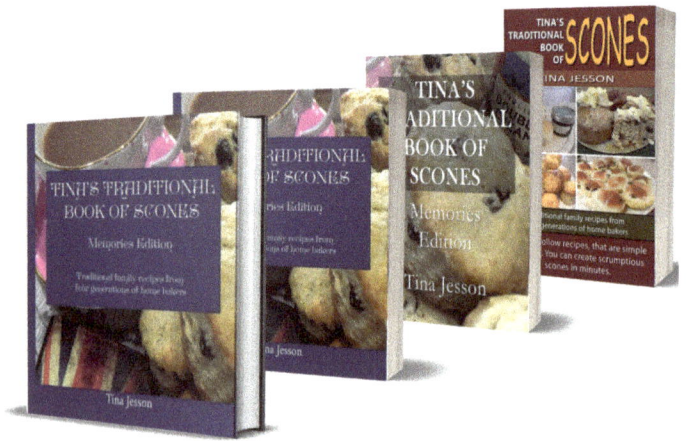

After you have collected and recorded your family recipes, then get them professionally published with a glossy cover, in hardback or paperback.

A priceless memento for you, a wonderful gift for your family.

Publish privately, or make it available to purchase worldwide.

FIND OUT MORE FROM

LionessPublishing.com/my-family-recipes

www.ingramcontent.com/pod-product-compliance
Lightning Source LLC
Chambersburg PA
CBHW060936170426
43194CB00026B/2971